■ SCHOLASTIC
News
Nonfiction Readers

Animal Life Cycles

Fascinating Facts About 6 Different Animal Life Cycles

by
Pam Zollman

D1714409

Children's Press®
A Division of Scholastic Inc.
New York Toronto London Auckland Sydney
Mexico City New Delhi Hong Kong
Danbury, Connecticut

Special thanks to the Kansas City Zoo and Omaha's Henry Doorly Zoo

Photo Credits:

Photographs © 2006: Animals Animals: 129 top right (Patricia Caulfield), 84, 85, 89 top right (Peter Gould/OSF), 124 (George H. Huey), 130 top left (Marie Read), 88 top left (Ralph Reinhold), 13 top right, 16 (Norbert Rosing), 130 bottom left (Viola's Photo Visions, Inc.); Brian Kenney: 114; Charlton Photos/Leigh Charlton: 32 top, 33 bottom right, 44, 45, 49 top right; Corbis Images: 113 bottom right, 117 top (Darrell Gulin), 37 (Julie Habel), 30 top left (Robert Pickett), 33 bottom left, 47 top (Premium Stock), 129 bottom left (Kevin Schafer), 13 bottom left, 17 (Scott T. Smith), 130 bottom right (Chase Swift), 128 right center, 129 top left (Kennan Ward), 130 top right (Lawson Wood); Dan Suzio Photography: 91, 92 bottom, 93 top right, 93 bottom left, 94, 95, 96, 98, 99, 100, 101, 105, 108, 109; Dembinsky Photo Assoc.: 28 top right, 29 top left (Dominique Braud), 63 (Jesse Cancelmo), 70 top left (E. R. Degginger), 92 top, 102 (DPA), back cover top left, 28 bottom right, 29 top right (Bill Lea), 83 (Gary Meszaros), 30 bottom left, 107 top (Skip Moody), 112 bottom left, 113 top, 115, 122, 123 (A. B. Sheldon); Dwight R. Kuhn Photography: front cover, back cover bottom left and center, 31 right, 32 bottom, 33 top left, 36, 38, 39, 40, 41, 42, 43, 48 center left, 48 top left, 48 bottom, 49 center right, 49 bottom, 50 top left, 50 bottom right, 71, 72, 73, 74, 75, 77, 78, 86, 87, 88 top right, 88 bottom left, 89 bottom, 89 top left, 90 top left, 90 bottom right, 93 bottom right, 93 top left, 97, 103, 107 bottom, 110 bottom left, 110 top right; Lynn and Donna Rogers: 12 bottom left, 13 bottom right, 24, 25, 29 bottom left, 29 center right; Marine Themes/Kelvin Aitken: back cover top right, 51, 68 bottom, 68 top, 69; Michael Durham/www.Durmphoto.com: 110 top left; Minden Pictures: 12 top, 19 (Jim Brandenburg), 23 (Matthias Breiter), 111, 121, 126, 129 center right (Frans Lanting), 12 bottom right, 15 (Yva Momatiuk/John Eastcott), 125 (Mike Parry), back cover bottom right (Norbert Wu); National Geographic Image Collection: 119 (Brian J. Skerry), 112 top, 120 (Steve Winter); Nature Picture Library Ltd.: 53 top right, 58 (Jurgen Freund), 79 (Duncan McEwan), 70 bottom left (Constantinos Petrinos); Peter Arnold Inc.: 128 bottom right (Reinhard Dirscherl/Bilderberg), 81 (Hans Pfletschinger); Photo Researchers, NY: 33 top right, 47 bottom, 48 top right, 49 top left (Chris Bjornberg), 13 top left, 21 (Tom Bledsoe), 90 top right (Dante Fenolio), 70 top right (Mark Harmel), 127, 128 top left (Rudiger Lehnen), 11, 27 (Jeff Lepore), 30 top right (Steve & Dave Maslowski), 50 top right (Tom McHugh), 35 (Will & Deni McIntyre), 128 center left (Alexis Rosenfeld), 28 center right (Len Rue Jr.); PictureQuest/Digital Vision: 50 bottom left; Seapics.com: 52 bottom left, 64 (Phillip Colla), 53 bottom left, 59 (Mark Conlin), 52 top right, 67 bottom (David B. Fleetham), 53 top left, 56 (Howard Hall), 52 bottom right, 53 bottom right, 55, 57, 61, 68 center left, 70 bottom right (Doug Perrine), 90 bottom left (Tim Rock), 65 (Masa Ushioda), 67 top (James D. Watt); Tom & Pat Leeson: 110 bottom right; Visuals Unlimited: 28 top left (Bill Banaszewski), 112 bottom right, 113 bottom left, 117 bottom (Ken Lucas), 30 bottom right (Joe McDonald).

0-516-24555-4 (trade bindup)

1 2 3 4 5 6 7 8 9 10 R 15 14 13 12 11 10 09 08 07 06

CHAPTER 1

A Bear Cub Grows Up

CHAPTER 2

A Chick Grows Up

A Shark Grows Up

CHAPTER 4

A Spiderling Grows Up

A Tadpole Grows Up

A Turtle Hatchling Grows Up

A Bear Cub Grows Up

WORD HUNT

Look for these words as you read. They will be in **bold**.

climb
(klime)

hibernate
(**hye**-bur-nate)

mammal
(**mam**-uhl)

12

cub
(kuhb)

den
(den)

nurse
(nurs)

rake
(rayk)

Bear Cubs!

A bear is a **mammal**.

Mammals have hair and give birth to babies.

A baby bear is called a **cub.**

Do you know when a bear cub is born?

bear cubs

A mother bear makes a **den** in the winter.

One or more cubs are born in the den.

The mother bear **nurses** her babies.

She keeps them warm, too.

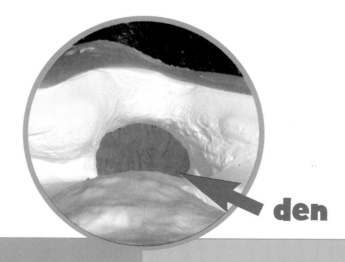

den

These bear cubs are nursing.
They are feeding on their mother's milk.

Now it is spring!

The bears go outside.

The cubs like to run and **climb** trees.

They can climb very high.

What are these cubs doing?

They are watching their mother.

She teaches them how to find food.

They copy everything she does.

Mother bear teaches her cubs how to catch fish.

Cubs learn what is good to eat.

They like nuts and fruits.

Fish and bugs taste good, too.

Cubs eat a lot and get fat.

This cub is eating a fish. Yum!

Now it is fall. It is time to get ready for winter.

The cubs help their mother **rake** leaves for beds.

Winter comes.

Mother bear and her cubs **hibernate**, or sleep.

hibernate

These cubs are raking
leaves to make a bed.

Spring comes again.

The bears come outside.

Most bear cubs will grow up by fall.

Soon, each bear will start a new family.

A BEAR CUB GROWS UP!

1 It is fall. Mother bear finds a den to hibernate. She will give birth to cubs in the winter.

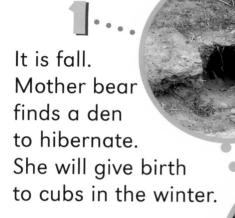

2 Mother bear and her cubs wake up in the spring.

3 Cubs learn what to eat and how to hunt in the summer.

7 Now it is summer.
This cub is a fully grown bear now.

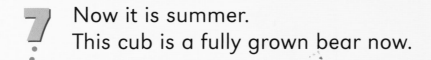

6 It is spring again. The cubs are almost grown-up. They will leave their mother soon.

5 Mother bear and her cubs hibernate during the winter.

4 It is time to get ready for winter. The cubs rake leaves into a den.

WHAT ELSE HIBERNATES?

A ladybug!

A skunk!

A toad!

A woodchuck!

CHAPTER 2

A Chick Grows Up

WORD HUNT

Look for these words as you read. They will be in **bold**.

comb
(kohm)

down
(down)

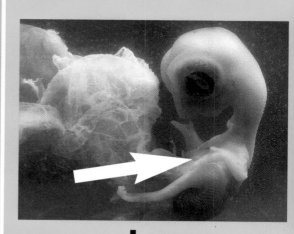

embryo
(**em**-bree-oh)

hatch

(hach)

hen

(hen)

rooster

(**roo**-stur)

wattle

(**wot**-uhl)

Peep! Peep!

Did you hear that?

This mother **hen** is with her chicks.

A chick is a bird.

A bird has feathers and lays eggs.

Do you know how a chick grows?

hen

chick

35

A hen lays eggs in a nest.

Some eggs have an **embryo** inside.

An embryo grows into a chick in 21 days.

embryo

eggs

This chick wants to **hatch**.

How will it get out?

It cracks open the shell with its egg tooth.

The egg tooth is on the chick's beak.

beak

Look! This chick is hatching.

A chick is wet when it hatches.

A chick has feathers called **down**.

The down will dry fast.

The chick is almost out of the egg.

Look! The down is dry.

These chicks are dry
and fluffy.

They can walk right away.

dry
down

Chicks like to eat seeds, bugs, and worms.

Chicks grow more feathers in about four weeks.

A **comb** grows on the chick's head.

A **wattle** grows under the chick's beak.

Is this chick grown yet?

comb

wattle

This chick is five weeks old.

Chicks are fully grown in six months.

Some chicks grow up to be **roosters**.

Other chicks grow up to be hens.

The hens will lay more eggs.

A rooster is a male, or boy, chicken.

A hen is a female, or girl, chicken.

47

A CHICK GROWS UP!

1 ··· ·
This embryo is only 10 days old.

2 ···
The embryo grows into a chick in 21 days. Look! It's hatching.

3 ····
It can take up to a day for a chick to hatch. Watch it go!

7 Some chicks grow up to be hens, like this one.

6 Watch it grow! It is 5 weeks old.

5 Soon they are dry and fluffy. This chick is 1 day old.

4 Chicks are wet when they hatch. This chick is almost out.

49

These Birds Hatch From Eggs, Too!

duck

goose

peacock

turkey

50

CHAPTER 3

A Shark Pup Grows Up

WORD HUNT

Look for these words as you read. They will be in **bold**.

adult
(**ah**-duhlt)

fish
(fish)

gill slit
(gil slit)

egg case
(eg kays)

embryo
(**em**-bree-oh)

hatch
(hach)

pouch
(pouch)

Shark Pups!

What is a shark pup?

A shark pup is a baby shark.

Sharks are **fish**. Fish live in water. They have fins and gills.

The **gill slits** are openings to the gills.

gill slit

fins

Sharks breathe through gills.
The gills are under the gill slits.

Do you know how a shark pup is born?

Some sharks **hatch** from eggs. Hard cases cover the eggs.

Some **egg cases** look like **pouches** or bags.

Some egg cases look like screws.

egg case

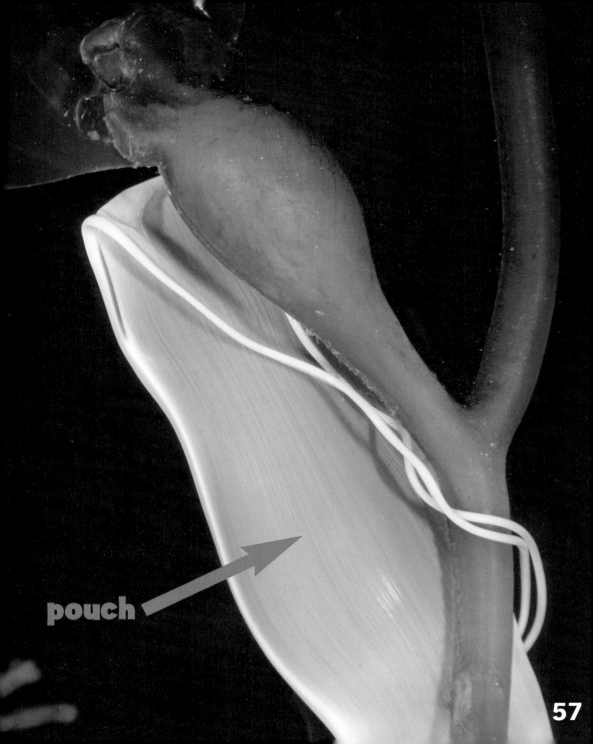

pouch

A shark **embryo** grows inside each egg case.

How does the pup hatch?

The pup uses its sharp teeth to break open the egg case.

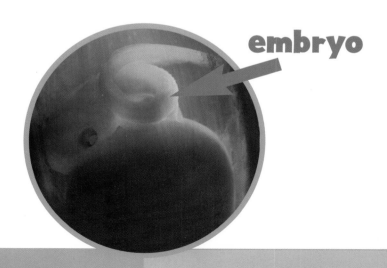

embryo

Look! This shark pup is coming out of its egg case.

Most shark pups do
not hatch from eggs.

They grow inside
their mother.

A shark pup can swim
when it is born.

Watch out, pups!

Bigger sharks might eat you.

Pups swim fast to get away.

Their tails push them through the water.

This shark may be looking for food. Watch out, pups!

Do you know what hungry pups eat?

Pups eat crabs and fish.

They eat clams and squid, too.

fish

This shark pup may eat some of these fish.

There are many kinds of shark pups.

They grow up to be **adult** sharks.

Then they can have pups of their own.

This is an adult
Whale shark.

This is an adult
Great White shark.

67

A Shark Pup Grows Up!

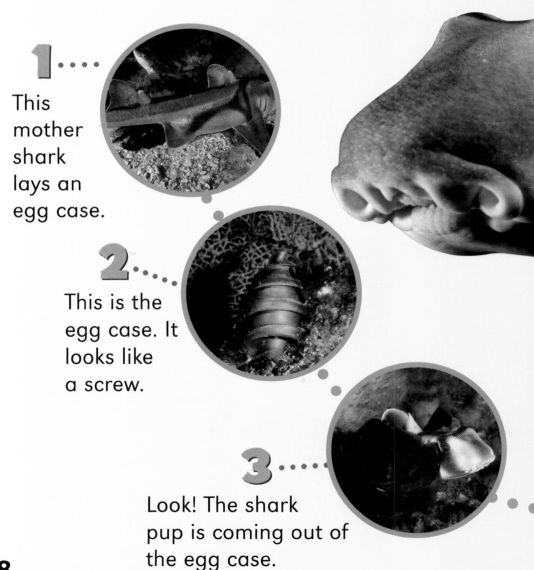

1 · · · ·
This mother shark lays an egg case.

2 · · · · ·
This is the egg case. It looks like a screw.

3 · · · · ·
Look! The shark pup is coming out of the egg case.

6 Look! It is an adult shark now.

5 The shark pup is growing.

4 The pup is out of its egg case now.

WHAT ELSE LIVES IN THE OCEAN?

A clam!

A jellyfish!

A sea horse!

A squid!

70

CHAPTER 4

A Spiderling Grows Up

WORD HUNT

Look for these words as you read. They will be in **bold**.

adult
(**ah**-duhlt)

moult
(mohlt)

sac
(sak)

arachnid
(uh-**rak**-nid)

eggs
(egz)

silk
(silk)

spiderling
(**spy**-dur-ling)

Spiderlings!

What are **spiderlings**?

Spiderlings are baby spiders.

Spiders are **arachnids**.

Arachnids have eight legs.

arachnid

These are spiderlings.

Spiderlings come from **eggs**.

A mother spider lays the eggs.

Then it wraps the eggs in a **sac**.

The sac keeps the eggs safe.

This mother spider is wrapping its eggs in a sac.

Some spiders hide their egg sacs.

Spiders use leaves to hide the sacs.

Some spiders sit with their sacs.

Some spiders carry their sacs.

egg sac

This spider is sitting with its egg sac. The sac is hidden under a leaf.

The eggs hatch inside the sac.

The spiderlings **moult**, or shed their skin, before they come out of the sac.

Then they use their fangs to cut open the sac.

Fangs are special teeth.

Look! Spiderlings are coming out of the sac.

Some spiderlings live on their own.

Some ride on their mother's back.

Some mother spiders die when the eggs hatch.

Some spiderlings eat their mother's body after it dies.

Yuck!

These spiderlings are riding on their mother's back.

All spiderlings spin **silk**.

Some make silk bridges.

Some glide away on silk strands.

Where are these spiderlings going?

They are going to make new homes.

silk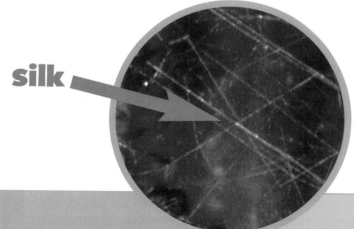

These spiderlings are gliding away on silk strands.

The spiderlings moult a few more times.

That means they shed their skin again.

Now they are **adult** spiders.

a spider
moulting

This spider is all grown-up!

A SPIDERLING GROWS UP!

1

In the fall, a female garden spider lays eggs. It makes a silk sac to protect the eggs.

2

The eggs grow in the sac. The spider hides the sac under a leaf to keep it safe.

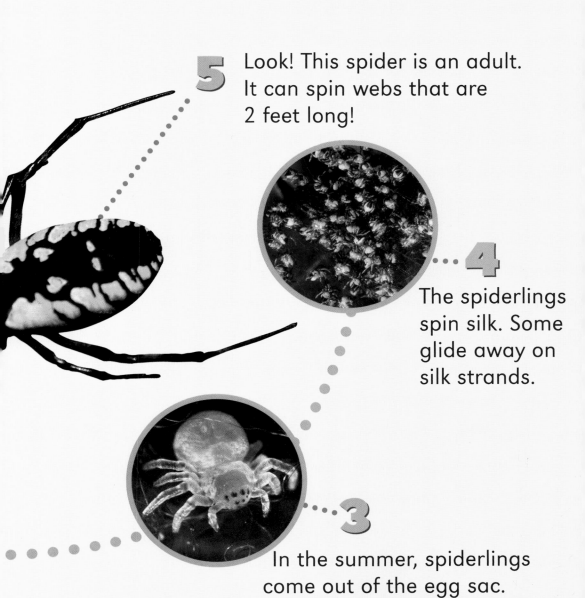

5 Look! This spider is an adult. It can spin webs that are 2 feet long!

4 The spiderlings spin silk. Some glide away on silk strands.

3 In the summer, spiderlings come out of the egg sac. There can be 800 spiderlings!

THESE ANIMALS HATCH FROM EGGS, TOO!

chicken

frog

shark

turtle

CHAPTER 5

A Tadpole Grows Up

WORD HUNT

Look for these words as you read. They will be in **bold**.

algae
(**al**-jee)

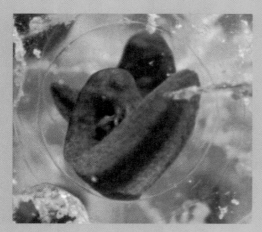

embryo
(**em**-bree-oh)

string
(string)

amphibian
(am-**fib**-ee-uhn)

blob
(blahb)

tadpole
(**tad**-pole)

worm
(wurm)

Tadpoles!

Are those fish?

No, they are **tadpoles**.

Tadpoles grow into frogs or toads.

tadpoles

These tadpoles will grow into toads.

Frogs and toads
are **amphibians**.

Amphibians live in water
and on land.

Frogs have smooth skin.

Toads have bumpy skin.

bump

toad

Look at the smooth skin on this frog.

Toads and frogs lay eggs in lakes, ponds, and puddles.

Frogs lay eggs in a **blob**.

Toads lay eggs in a **string**.

Jelly covers the eggs to keep them safe.

frog egg blob

Toad eggs look
like strings.

Embryos grow inside the eggs.

The eggs will hatch in about 2 to 3 weeks.

The embryos become tadpoles when they hatch.

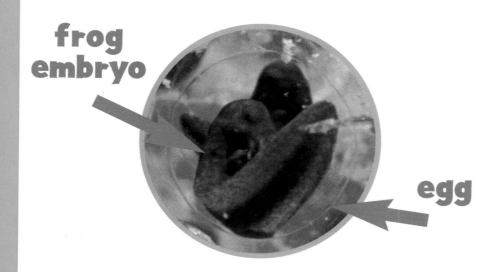

frog embryo

egg

Look! These frog eggs will hatch soon.

A tadpole looks like a fish.

It has a tail, but no legs.

Its gills help it get air from the water.

It eats **algae**. Algae are plants that live in water.

algae

This frog tadpole is swimming in algae.

What is happening to this tadpole?

It is growing back legs.

Its front legs will grow later.

Its lungs are growing, too.

Its lungs help it to breathe air.

legs

105

Three months have passed.

The tadpole has lost its tail.

It's time to hop out
of the water!

The tadpole eats bugs
and **worms** now.

Tadpoles can grow into toads.

Tadpoles can grow into frogs.

107

A Tadpole Grows Up!

1 Jelly covers the eggs to keep the frog eggs safe. Embryos are inside the eggs.

2 Look! This egg is about to hatch. When the egg hatches, a tadpole comes out.

3 These tadpoles are 10 days old.

7 Where's the tail? It's gone! The tadpole is grown up. It is a frog now.

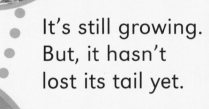

6

It's still growing. But, it hasn't lost its tail yet.

5

The tadpole is getting bigger. It has back legs now!

4

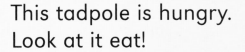

This tadpole is hungry. Look at it eat!

THESE ANIMALS LAY EGGS IN THE WATER, TOO!

jellyfish

newt

salamander

trout

CHAPTER 6

A Turtle Hatchling Grows Up

WORD HUNT

Look for these words as you read. They will be in **bold**.

egg
(eg)

hatchling
(**hach**-ling)

shell
(shel)

egg tooth
(eg tooth)

hatch
(hach)

tortoise
(**tor**-tuhss)

turtle
(**tur**-tuhl)

Hatchlings!

Have you ever seen a baby **turtle**?

It is called a **hatchling**.

Baby **tortoises** look like baby turtles. They are called hatchlings, too.

tortoise hatchling

This turtle hatchling is coming out of an egg.

Tortoises are turtles that live on land.

A tortoise has a high, round **shell**.

Turtles that live in water have a low, flat shell.

shell

This turtle's shell is low and flat.

This tortoise's shell is high and round.

shell

117

Sea turtles spend most of their time in the water.

Female sea turtles swim to the same beach every year.

They go there to lay eggs.

Look at this sea turtle swim!

This sea turtle mother digs a hole in the sand.

She lays **eggs** in the hole.

She covers the eggs with sand.

Then she goes back to the water.

eggs

This sea turtle mother is digging a hole. She will lay eggs in it.

121

The eggs **hatch** in a few months.

The hatchlings have an **egg tooth**.

They use it to open the soft shells of their eggs.

Then the turtles come out.

egg tooth

Look! The turtle hatchling used its egg tooth to open the egg.

Sea turtle hatchlings go to the water.

They eat jellyfish.

Tortoise hatchlings stay on land.

They eat grasses and plants.

tortoise hatchling

These sea turtle hatchlings are going to the water.

All hatchlings look like their parents.

They are just smaller.

It takes years for them to grow up.

sea turtle hatchling

This sea turtle is grown-up.

A Turtle Hatchling Grows Up!

1····
A mother
sea turtle
swims to
a beach.

2···
She digs a hole.
Then she lays eggs.

3····
She covers the eggs
with sand.

7 Now the sea turtle is grown-up.

6 The turtle hatchling is growing! It eats jellyfish, turtle grass, and other things.

5 Now the turtle hatchling goes to the water.

4 Look! An egg is hatching. It's a sea turtle hatchling.

THESE ANIMALS HAVE SHELLS, TOO!

armadillo

crab

scallop

snail

YOUR NEW WORDS

adult (**ah**-duhlt) a person or animal that is grown-up

algae (**al**-jee) very tiny plants that grow in water that do not have roots or stems

amphibian (am-**fib**-ee-uhn) an animal that hatches in water

arachnid (uh-**rak**-nid) an animal that has eight legs and two body parts

blob (blahb) a frog lays a group, or blob of eggs

climb (klime) bears climb, or go up, trees

comb (kohm) bright red skin on a chick's head

cub (kuhb) animals like baby lions, wolves, and bears are cubs

den (den) a cave or hollow tree where bears sleep during the winter

down (down) the feathers that cover the chick's body

egg (eg) a round or oval shell in which a baby grows

egg case (eg kays) a layer around an egg that keeps it safe

egg tooth (eg tooth) a sharp tooth that a hatchling uses to open its egg

eggs (egz) oval or round objects in which baby birds, reptiles, and fish grow and change

embryo (**em**-bree-oh) a baby that is growing inside an egg or in its mother

fish (fish) an animal that lives in water and has fins, and gills

gill slit (gil slit) gill slits cover a fish's gills

hatch (hach) to break out of an egg

hatchling (**hach**-ling) a baby animal that hatches from an egg

hen (hen) a female, or girl, chicken

hibernate (hye-bur-nate) to sleep through
the winter

mammal (mam-uhl) a warm-blooded
animal that nurses its babies
and is covered with hair

moult (mohlt) to shed skin

nurse (nurs) to feed a baby its
mother's milk

pouch (pouch) a bag

rake (rayk) bears rake, or collect, leaves
to make beds

rooster (**roo**-stur) a male, or boy, chicken

sac (sak) a bag made of spider silk that holds spider eggs

shell (shel) a hard or soft covering

silk (silk) thin strings that spiders make; spiderlings use them for gliding and making bridges

spiderling (**spy**-dur-ling) a baby spider

string (string) a toad lays a string of eggs

tadpole (**tad**-pole) a young frog or toad that lives in water, breathes through gills, and has a tail, but no legs

tortoise (**tor**-tuhss) a turtle that lives on land

turtle (**tur**-tuhl) a kind of reptile that lives on land and in water

wattle (**wot**-uhl) bright red skin that hangs under a chick's beak

worm (wurm) a small animal that lives in the soil

INDEX

FIND OUT MORE

Books:

All About Frogs, by Jim Arnosky (Scholastic Press, 2002)

Chicks and Chickens, by Gail Gibbons (Holiday House, 2003)

Eyewitness: Shark, by Miranda MacQuitty (DK Publishing, 2004)

Face to Face: Frogs, Scholastic Inc., 2001

Face to Face with the Chicken, by Christian Havard (Charlesbridge Publishing, 2003)

Life Cycle of a Spider, by Ron Fridell and Patricia Walsh (Heinemann Library, 2001)

Sea Turtles, by Carol K. Lindeen (Capstone Press, 2005)

See Through: Reptiles, by Steve Parker (Running Press Kids, 2003)

Shark, by Simon Mugford (Scholastic, 2004)

Spiders, by Claire Llewellyn (Franklin Watts, 2002)

Spinning Spiders, by Ruth Berman (Lerner Publications, 1998)

The Trouble With Tadpoles: a first look at the life cycle of a frog, by Sam Goodwin; illustrated by Simone Abel (Picture Window Books, 2005)

Watch Me Grow: Bear, by Lisa Magloff (DK Publishing, 2003)

Websites:

http://www.americanbear.org/Cubscomer.htm

http://www.enchantedlearning.com/coloring/lifecycles.shtml

http://www.enchantedlearning.com/subjects/amphibians/Frog/

http://www.enchantedlearning.com/subjects/arachnids/spider/

http://www.enchantedlearning.com/subjects/birds/info/chicken/

http://www.enchantedlearning.com/subjects/mammals/bear/

http://www.enchantedlearning.com/subjects/sharks/

http://www.tortoise-tracks.org/gopherus/lifecycle.html

http://www.nationalgeographic.com/kids/activities/index.html

http://www.nationalgeographic.com/kids/creative_feature/

http://www.nationalgeographic.com/0010/brownbears2.html

http://www.nationalgeographic.com/0203/frogs.html

http://www.nationalgeographic.com/0206/sharks.html

MEET THE AUTHOR

Pam Zollman is the award-winning author of short stories, articles, and books for kids. She is the author of *North Dakota* (Scholastic/Children's Press) and the other Life Cycle books in this series. She lives in rural Pennsylvania where she has seen bears much closer than she would like; where she can watch chicken eggs hatch; where there are no sharks; where she likes to watch spiders grow up in her backyard; has played with tadpoles, toads, and frogs; and once had a pet turtle.